My Reminders... Reflections of a Fledgling Buddhist

I0558830

Sue Goodwin

Wisdom of Life Series

Learning Moments Press
Oakmont, PA

My Reminders…Reflections of a Fledgling Buddhist
Published by Learning Moments Press
Oakmont, PA 15139

ISBN-13: 979-8-9860800-7-9

BISAC Subject
OCC010000 Body/Mind & Spirit/Mindfulness & Meditation
OCC000000 Body/Mind & Spirit/General

ONIX Code: 01 General/Adult

Book Layout:
Mike Murray, pearhouse.com

To Ryan, Scott, Jason, and Kate

To My Spiritual Friends

Table of Contents

Introductory Note

Spiritual practice is often an upstream journey. It requires courage to break free from the habitual patterns of our minds and patience to persevere, even when progress seems elusive. Each individual's spiritual growth is unique, and Upekha's[1] introductory notes and selected quotations reflect one person's journey to understand and follow the teachings of the Buddha. It is fascinating to see how she relates these quotes to her personal experiences. Such reflections are a powerful way to internalize what we have read or learned from others, and it is through this process that we can grow spiritually. I hope that this collection of quotations and Upekha's reflections will inspire many readers to internalize spiritual wisdom in their own unique ways.

When I asked Upekha to send reminders for our meditation sessions, I never imagined that such an ordinary

---

[1]   Upekha is Sue Goodwin's Buddhist name.

task would lead to a project as meaningful as this. I deeply appreciate her efforts in finding appropriate quotes and consistently sending reminders. I am extremely grateful that her dedication not only helped many people sustain their meditation practice but also resulted in this inspiring account of gradual spiritual progress.

May this work inspire and encourage many to walk their spiritual journey with confidence.

Bhante Pemaratana
Chief Monk, Pittsburgh Buddhist Center

My Introduction to Buddhism

I was introduced to Buddhism in 2007 while working on the first Obama campaign. That's when I met Jonnie, our local campaign leader who was a practicing Buddhist. She had a long history of helping monks in the Pittsburgh area and beyond. On countless nights, monks would arrive at her house, tired and hungry, on their way to a distant monastery or an event somewhere in the South. In a day or two they resumed their journey, well fed and rested. But before leaving, they shared teachings and practices with her and anyone she may have invited to meet them. More than once, it was I.

Jonnie also introduced me to Bhante Pemaratana, commonly known as Bhante Pema, a young Theravadan monk who had recently joined the new Pittsburgh Buddhist Center. I learned then that "Bhante" is an honorific title used to address monks, similar to how Catholics refer to priests as "Father." I was immediately drawn to this reserved, yet friendly Sri Lankan monk with an infectious smile and warm demeanor. He was soon joined by two additional monks, the three of them making their home in a 1600 square foot house they had converted into a humble Buddhist temple.

Recently retired and with time on my hands, I was ready to begin exploring my spirituality. Thus began a relationship with the Pittsburgh Buddhist Center now in its seventeenth year.

My Deepening Involvement

In addition to attending weekly meditation sessions, I began participating in workshops and monthly events. As a former English teacher, I enjoyed tutoring new monks as they arrived, mostly helping them adapt their proper British grammar to "American English." My one-on-one time with them provided opportunities for me to ask questions and observe how they went about their daily lives.

In 2017, the monks began offering meditation sessions at local libraries. As attendance grew, Bhante Pema started sending out weekly email reminders. The reminder was boilerplate—date, time, location. Soon, he included a motivational quotation meant to assist attendees in learning more about the benefits of meditation while also encouraging them with their practice.

Over the years, attendance at the Center had increased, Bhante Pema began working on his doctorate at a local university, and all three monks had expanded their roles in the community. Knowing how busy they were, I volunteered to help in any way I could. Bhante suggested that I assume responsibility for sending out the weekly reminder to the various meditation groups—a perfect job for me.

It was a clerical job, not seemingly geared to expanding my knowledge of Buddhism. But the act of choosing and collecting quotations provided me with unexpected opportunities for deep, personal reflection.

As I began thinking about which quotations to include, I returned to the books and essays I had read since I had begun studying Buddhism. I decided to avoid looking at collections of quotations on the internet. Without context, they often held little meaning for me. Instead, each morning I would spend a quiet hour reading, underlining, taking notes, and mining the rich texts for greater understanding. I then selected sentences and phrases that held important insights for me. Sometimes I chose quotations appropriate for a holiday or season of the year. More often I was drawn to quotations that spoke to me about an issue I was struggling with. This was particularly true as I navigated the complexities of the COVID pandemic. As time passed, I began to see how reading and reflecting deeply on the various quotations helped to clarify my understanding of many aspects of the Buddha's teachings.

My Decision to Write

Over the course of six years, I had accumulated more than 200 quotations. At some point, the idea of compiling my favorites occurred to me. At first, I wasn't quite sure what purpose such a collection would serve, or who, if anyone, would find it interesting. Then I began to think about my grandchildren. Perhaps as I near my 80th year, I might want to share with them some bits of wisdom that have helped me cope with life's uncertainties. Or, reading the quotations that have mattered to me might let them come to know me differently, maybe more fully.

From this initial, highly personal impulse, the possibility of creating a book for a wider audience began to emerge. We live in such stressful times, perhaps others might find some comfort in these words that have inspired me. I also wanted to present my story of gathering and contemplating the quotations as one unexpected way of interacting with Buddhist thinking. Being fully aware of my continuing status as a beginning student, I want to emphasize that none of what I have included here is intended to represent a final or even deep understanding of the concepts I have addressed. I view it as a testimony to being open to any form of contact with Buddhist teachings that might present itself. And it is simply a part of my story.

With this in mind, I began to sort through my computer file labeled "Reminders," selecting a random assortment of quotations that held meaning for me. As I gathered my favorite quotations together, I thought it would be helpful to the reader if they were presented in some sort of organized pattern. They covered a broad spectrum of topics, and I believed this might help in understanding them. For months, I labored over what that organizational structure might be.

I began looking at the content of the quotations, clustering them thematically. There were many on generosity and greed, meditation, mindfulness, love, suffering and morality. Somehow, arranging them in little boxes didn't seem true to the Buddha's intent. I'm not sure why, but I eventually found myself revisiting his first teaching after his enlightenment. Surprisingly, I found that these little clusters of quotes that I had compiled all referred back to that teaching which today is known as *The Four Noble Truths.*

The fourth truth presents the path to enlightenment along which I was able to place many of my quotations that addressed concepts like "intention," "consciousness," and "effort." I was beginning to see a common thread which was about to help me satisfy my desire for some structure.

Finding answers in *The Four Noble Truths* comes as somewhat of a surprise. My relationship with that teaching did not begin well. After first reading it, I was left feeling that Buddhism sounded pessimistic. The main theme of suffering and how we struggle through life was woven through not only this discourse, but many of the early teachings I encountered.

It was only after I realized that through translations of the original Pali records and later written texts, a new

Buddhist learner might miss the full range of the Buddha's message. The Pali word "dukkha" is most often translated into English to mean suffering, but the Buddha's usage of "dukkha" suggests a more multifaceted meaning. It includes dissatisfaction, disappointment, longing, and regret. Once I was able to recognize the full scope of the nature of "dukkha," *The Four Noble Truths* became more inviting to me. My initial thoughts of pessimism were replaced with ones of opportunity, choice, and personal growth.

I have learned from this experience to be cautious with translations, to study, whenever possible, with monks who understand the subtleties of the Pali language and can help steer students through readings that may not always clearly reflect layers of meaning. I eventually found great comfort and optimism in this first teaching of the Buddha.

Before going any further, it might be helpful to include an orientation to the life of the Buddha and a brief introduction to *The Four Noble Truths*, the Buddha's first teaching after his enlightenment.

The Four Noble Truths

Before he was known as the Buddha or Awakened One, he was a young prince named Siddhartha who lived in India. It was common at the time for some intellectuals and religious leaders to leave their homes and become wandering ascetics in search of answers to many of life's age-old mysteries.

The young prince, troubled by the suffering he saw in the world, left his family and a luxurious lifestyle hoping that through deep meditation he would find the way to eliminate suffering from people's lives.

He traveled the countryside for many years and studied with several master sages in his attempts to answer questions regarding the origin of suffering and how we can overcome it, before finally, through deep meditation, experiencing a fully enlightened mind. For the next 45 years he wandered by foot through India and neighboring countries, teaching. During that time, he amassed thousands of disciples and, it is believed, offered as many as 84,000 teachings. He was called "the Buddha" by his followers, which means, the "Enlightened" or "Awakened" one.

Once enlightened, he decided to share the many revelations he had on suffering and the nature of reality. He offered in his first teaching, *The Four Noble Truths* that:

1. Suffering and dissatisfaction exist in the world. We are born, grow old, become ill, and die. Along the way, continually searching for happiness, we are met with disappointment, dissatisfaction, and sorrow.

2. Greed and its partners, hatred and delusion (ignorance), are the causes of our suffering.

3. A solution exists to defeat suffering, and in the process, understand the nature of reality.

4. That solution is found in following an eight-step path describing how the development of proper moral or ethical conduct, mental discipline, and wisdom can lead to the cessation of suffering.

The Buddha then went on to lay out three components of the *Noble Eightfold Path*, the fourth and final section of *The Four Noble Truths*. He describes the three, along with their eight actions as follows.

Ethical Conduct consisting of:

> *Right Action* - refrain from harming others, stealing, and engaging in sexual misconduct.
>
> *Right Speech* - avoid hateful, untruthful, and harmful speech or gossip.
>
> *Right livelihood* - engage in making a living in ways that benefit living beings, not by inflicting harm on them.

Mental Discipline consisting of:

> *Right Effort* - recognize negative states that can potentially arise and work hard to maintain positive states in their place.

> *Right Mindfulness* - develop mindfulness of the body, feelings, mind, and teachings of the Buddha.
>
> *Right Concentration* - develop skills of deep meditation through which we can achieve an understanding of the nature of reality.

Wisdom consisting of:

> *Right View* - recognize ignorance and how our mistaken views of finding happiness in permanent or material sources keep us floundering in cycles of suffering.
>
> *Right Intention* - avoid thoughts of attachment and harmful   intent.

Upon the Buddha's death, 300 monks gathered to share oral records of his teachings which have been preserved and today make up the canon of what is now referred to as Buddhism.

My Learning from the Quotations

As I sifted through the quotations I had accumulated, I discovered that without exception I was able to relate each one of them to *The Four Noble Truths.* It became clear to me that everything the Buddha taught after that first lesson was closely linked to it and led to deeper explanations of the nature of existence. This discovery represented a major "aha moment" for me, who by previously learning various concepts and lessons discreetly, missed seeing the connecting bridges linking them all. It's through that bridging, I discovered, that each concept gains clarity and importance.

This realization became a key means for me to significantly understand the comprehensiveness of *The Four Noble Truths*. By connecting the quotations in some way to *The Four Noble Truths*, I was learning that there are no boundaries in Buddhism. No boundaries between me and the rest of humanity, no boundaries between humanity and the rest of nature.

I was also able to recognize the dangers of isolating Buddhist concepts when studying them. Periodically, as my practice grows, I need to step back and view the totality of the Buddha's thinking, viewing it like a dynamic web made up of interrelated, supporting threads.

The westernization of teaching mindfulness might be a good example of how when one Buddhist concept is plucked from the body of teachings it can lose its original meaning or effectiveness.

Western writings often treat mindfulness as a self-help tool designed to increase productivity or improve concentration. Shifting the Buddhist focus of using our mindfulness from serving others to increasing productivity represents a distortion of the Buddha's thinking. The study of mindfulness removed from the context of Buddhist teachings as a whole can easily result in such distortion.

The fact I came upon this new perspective of the Buddha's teachings in such an unconventional way is itself important. My experience with the quotations represents a distinct discovery, one that expanded my awareness of things I thought I already knew. Not knowing the varied ways of interacting with Buddhist thought, but being open to the possibility that something unique might await us, can lead to new learning and growth. That discovery is important enough to me that I share it.

I finally decided to present the quotations randomly, the same way they were presented to the Buddhist Center's meditators each week in their reminders. But like the meditators, some who were beginners and others, very experienced, the quotations speak to different people in different ways.

For those who are not students of Buddhism, I suggest considering each quotation as its own entity, to enjoy and contemplate, maybe gaining some personal motivation or comfort.

For those who are beginning students of Buddhism, the quotations provide an opportunity to look more deeply into the connections each one might have to our lives, other Buddhist teachings, and ultimately back to *The Four Noble Truths.*

Buddhism does not ask us to accept any of the teachings on faith. The Buddha more than once stated that we should accept only those teachings that we can affirm with our own experience. If we don't understand them, we can put them aside until the time comes when we are able to relate to them through our lives. I came upon these connections quite accidentally and even though I have a deeper understanding of the body of the Buddha's work as a whole, there is much for me yet to learn.

Since many of the quotations included here are written by contemporary thinkers applying Buddhist concepts to COVID, political upheaval, or other current experiences, I often found them to be more relatable. I consciously made an effort to find life experiences in the quotations I selected, then discovered that with a little effort I was able to link them to *The Four Noble Truths.* This exercise helped me better understand the interrelatedness of all the teachings.

I have also included examples of how a few of my favorite quotations deepened my understanding of some key Buddhist concepts. I have used the following vignettes as an introduction to the random list. They are included as examples of my experience and ultimately some progress I may have made along the way.

Generosity/Greed

*Generosity brings happiness at every stage of
its expression: we experience joy in forming
the intention to give, we experience joy in the
action of giving, and we experience joy in
remembering that we have given.*

BETH ROTH, *"FAMILY DHAMMA:
THE JOY OF GENEROSITY"*

One of my favorite quotations is this one by Beth Roth in which she introduces us to the layers of joy we receive from practicing generosity. It has led me to investigate my own behavior, opening the door for me to see and experience the beauty of a simple generous act. Each time I read it, I am reminded of that first teaching of the Buddha's, where in *The Four Noble Truths*, he states that greed is the cause of suffering.

Greed originates as a feeling of not having enough, of having or being less than. It can progress to craving, a desire coupled with passion for things we do not have, power we want, or perhaps an ideal relationship beyond our reach. It finally can transform into attachment, the most destructive of the three, holding on at all costs to people, things, or ideas, believing they are the ultimate source of our happiness. Like the jealous husband or the political zealot moved to violence in his effort to preserve his beliefs.

These unfulfilled desires can often result in festering dissatisfaction and mental suffering.

Also, in his first teaching, the Buddha goes on to tell us that we can get rid of life's suffering and dissatisfaction, then outlines the eight-step path for doing so. Embedded in that path and repeated in many of his later discourses lies his explanation of the best way to combat greed—by practicing generosity.

Some Southeast Asian cultures believe that by nurturing generosity from early childhood, we can discover a direct path to enlightenment. Practicing conscious generosity becomes an early focus and goal of daily living. A visitor to a Southeast Asian country who compliments someone on a piece of clothing or decorative item in their home will often find the item offered to them as a gift.

Such actions can come as a surprise to many Westerners. The importance of generosity is often understated in how we describe Buddhism. It plays only a minor role in most Western writings.

While searching for quotations, I found many directly focused on generosity or on greed. From them I have learned to appreciate the simplicity and power of one generous act.

How, from the moment of intention, we experience that first inkling of satisfaction. It was because of Roth's quotation that I developed a curiosity about my experiences with generosity.

I returned to this notion of generosity over and over within the quotations, seeking new understanding. I practiced what I think is a form of meditation, concentrated lingering over examples of my experience with generosity—what I remember; how I felt when faced with either receiving or giving. I was able to recreate parts of my experiences. My clearest discovery was that there are two reciprocal roles present during an expression of generosity, both parties, giver and receiver, necessary in creating a shared joy.

Looking back, I was able to conclude that over the years I had adopted a pattern of rejecting the generosity of others. Until recently my reaction to a generous gesture had often been to discourage it. How often I have said, "Thank you, but you don't have to do that." Or simply, "Oh, you shouldn't have." When offered assistance, I might thank the person while proclaiming my ability to do the task myself. Perhaps such responses can be attributed to my attempts to prove myself capable. Or maybe they come from some quirky, American social norm that reflects our national pride in individualism and independence.

I was soon able to see how ungracious these responses are. Why would I deprive a person of the joy that comes from performing an act of generosity? This discovery led me to examine the relationship between giver and receiver more deeply along with the significance of the fleeting moment that finds them sharing an instant of mutual joy.

Verbally expressing that lived moment of joy remains difficult for me. I can most accurately say that it occurs 100% in the present… not one brain cell can be connected to either past or future while experiencing that rush of pure joy.

This personal example that occurred one winter illustrates the range of satisfaction that can radiate from a rather insignificant act.

During a fundraiser, the Buddhist Center sold handmade Christmas ornaments decorated with Buddhist images and designs (yes, the irony!). On a cold, wintry afternoon I was preparing to go to the Center to pick up the ornaments I had ordered when I received a call from another member of our *Sangha* (congregation) who lives near me. Dayna, who has MS and had avoided going out during the pandemic, asked if I minded picking up her ornaments as well. She would come for them at my home the next day. Of course, I agreed.

I selected six for myself and then chose six for Dayna. When I returned home, I called to let her know that I had them, adding that I got her the last ornament decorated with an image of the sitting Buddha, which, I added, was especially beautiful.

The next day she and her husband stopped by to pick up the ornaments. He came to the door while she remained in the car. As I handed him the box and walked outside with him to wave to Dayna, he opened it, removed the bright pink ornament adorned with the image of the sitting Buddha, and offered it to me saying, "Dayna wants you to have this one. She said you liked it."

I was about to open my mouth to utter, "Oh, no... this one is the most beautiful of them all. She should keep it." But then I looked up at the car and saw her face, nearly lost in the folds of her parka, intently watching our exchange. A broad smile crossed her face as I noticed her, from a side glance, anticipating my reaction. Thankfully, I had the awareness and presence of mind to say, "Thank you so much...what a wonderful gift!"

I looked up again and during that instant we, giver and receiver, were joined in a moment of mutual generosity. Then, just as quickly, we both waved as her husband entered the car, and they drove off.

That split second of a silent connection grew out of a simple act of generosity.

I understood that we each played shifting roles—once a giver, then, receiver. Had I not given her the opportunity to present that ornament by insisting she keep it for herself, she would have been robbed of the chance of giving it to me. The satisfaction that welled up inside of me because I made the correct response to her husband's offer left me feeling that I could indeed change a lifelong habit. At the same time, her act of remembering that I liked the ornament, then choosing to give it to me, touched me deeply.

From this singular moment of awareness of both of our actions, I have discovered that if I pay attention and am mindful of the people around me, I can experience similar moments more often. I am pleasantly surprised that I can influence the number and intensity of these moments by choosing generosity for others and myself. The moments may be fleeting; they may even be second hand, not involving me directly, but they are all around me. Each one remains and helps me feel a greater connection with others, while providing moments of genuine pleasure.

Not many quotations in this collection have made such an impact on me. But I realize how I have now been introduced to the proverbial iceberg, the tip of the potential learning that exists in Buddhist teachings and the many ways I can interact with them. I continue to revisit them all, knowing that one day when the need is there and my mind is ready, another might surface in a way that moves me to look longer and more deeply into its meaning.

Spiritual Friendship

*As iron sharpens iron, so one
person sharpens another.*

Proverbs 27:17, *The Bible*

*The Sangha is a refuge because those who have
preceded us on the path can give us advice on the
journey ahead, while those who are walking with
us can provide companionship on the journey,
bring us back to the path when we deviate, and
help us up when we stumble and fall.*

The Buddha, *from the Tipitaka*

At the Pittsburgh Buddhist Center we often speak of the role and importance of "spiritual friendship" in our development. We believe that through chanting together, meditating together, even working together, we are drawn more closely to the teachings of the Buddha. I can also add grieving together to this list. When our Buddhist

Center family tragically lost a beloved member, the pain was deep, intense and enduring, but this little family eventually found comfort and an expanded spiritual awareness through coming together in grief.

As an educator, I am intrigued by these two quotations which have led me to examine the meaning of the term "spiritual friendship" and how human connection continues to influence my learning. I love the brevity and implicit wisdom of the quote taken from the *Bible.* The notion of "sharpening" drew my attention, calling to mind that by sharpening, we hone and polish our efforts on whatever we choose to pursue. It reminds me of a close-knit group of women I've met at the Pittsburgh Buddhist Center and whom I've grown to love.

We are an unlikely group. Separated by age, ethnicity, careers, and backgrounds, but sharing the similarities of our Buddhist practice, we see ourselves in each other, understanding the private challenges we each face. I have seen the growth in each of us. Growth that is literally visible to the eye. Once when asked to describe the benefits of meditation, the Buddha listed "a beautiful complexion" among them. During the early days of dating my now husband, he had been struggling with severe back pain for several weeks. I didn't realize how much pain he was in until I later saw a photo of him taken at a party we had attended. The photo captured and preserved the shadowy lines etched deeply under his eyes that told the story of his suffering. Like him, the countenances of my female friends reflect their innermost being. I see on their faces their beauty and how it grows as their practice deepens.

It is not uncommon for people who are active in spiritual organizations to cling to these organizations too much, to attach and even compete for leadership roles. These women of Pittsburgh Buddhist Center are aware of that temptation and remind each other that what they do at the Center is performed as part of their practice. They are my spiritual friends.

I was also attracted to the Biblical quotation because it illustrates a unique feature of Buddhism, inclusivity and respectful acceptance of all religions. The Buddha, unlike many spiritual leaders, encouraged his followers not to leave their former religious sects to follow him, but to stay behind and continue learning from their leaders, gathering competing viewpoints before making their own decisions. That respect continues today in our *Sangha* which welcomes active practitioners from all faiths.

The second quotation addresses the notion of "spiritual friendship" more directly. One of the first things we learn and practice as beginning students of Buddhism is to take refuge in "The Triple Gem"—the Buddha, *Dhamma*, and *Sangha*. By doing so, we honor the Buddha as a person, how he lived, and what he stood for. The *Dhamma* consists of the vast body of his recorded teachings. The *Sangha* represents the community of monks and nuns who embody the teachings, carrying them from generation to generation while teaching and supporting those who embrace them.

(Modern interpretations of *Sangha* can refer to practitioners of a particular temple in addition to monks and nuns.) Taking refuge implies that we can go to the monks when we need guidance and direction, perhaps the purest example of the teacher-student relationship.

I have always maintained that the *Sangha* doesn't garner the same attention as the Buddha and *Dhamma* when discussing The Triple Gem. I believe it's because the source of most of the commentary and teaching comes from monks and too much praise or discussion of the *Sangha* might seem prideful to them. I know that during my early days of attending the Pittsburgh Buddhist Center, it was the *Sangha* which resided in our modest temple that kept me coming back.

From day one, it has been my fascination with the monks that drew me to Buddhism. It may have begun with the fact that they represented a new and enchanting culture, but the more I got to know them, the more I connected them to Buddhism and the more drawn to the teachings I became. Being with them in our temple and as they assimilated into our local communities, I was able to watch first-hand their compassion, acceptance, and affection for everyone they encountered.

The Buddha, in this quotation, made it perfectly clear that the living *Sangha*—the community of monks and nuns—was created by him not only to preserve the *Dhamma*, but to teach it and support those "with a little dust in their eyes," who understand just enough that they want more and are searching for learned teachers who offer guidance and support.

The monks of the Pittsburgh Buddhist Center, too, are my teachers and my spiritual friends.

As I continued thinking about what sets "spiritual friendship" apart, I came across a definition cited in Brene Brown's book, *Atlas of the Heart*, that further examines friendship and the importance of human bonding. In it, theorist, Judith Jordan distinguishes among different types of connection stating that:

> The need for connection in which growth is a priority, is the core motivation in people's lives. In growth-fostering relationships, people are able to bring themselves most fully and authentically into connection.

The addition of growth as a factor of friendship provided me with what I needed to distinguish "spiritual friendship" from its more general meaning. The monks motivate me by bringing to life the teachings of the Buddha through their interactions with the world and each other, showing me what I am capable of becoming while offering support for my efforts to move forward in the right direction. My fellow practitioners serve as conduits for understanding the *Dhamma* as I watch how they learn and grow. It is through my relationships with them that I am able to see defilements lessened, tolerance increased, and calmness presented where tension once resided. These are definitely "growth-fostering" relationships, safe and motivating, feeding my intention to sharpen or expand my practice.

Finally, I am including here a brief account of a conversation between the Buddha and his longtime personal attendant, Ananda, that further illustrates the importance of "spiritual friendship" and its direct connection to the *Four Noble Truths*.

> One day, Ananda and the Buddha were sitting alone on a hill together, overlooking the plains of the Ganges. Having served as the Buddha's attendant for many years, Ananda often shared his reflections and insights with him. This afternoon, Ananda spoke. "Dear respected teacher," Ananda said. "It seems to me that half of the spiritual life is good friendship, good companionship, good comradeship." (I imagine that Ananda said this with some level of confidence to praise the merits of spiritual friendship.) But the Buddha quickly corrected him: "Not so, Ananda, Not so." He continued, "This is the ENTIRE spiritual life, Ananda, that is, good friendship, good companionship, good comradeship. When a monk has a good friend, a good companion, a good comrade, it is to be expected that he will develop and cultivate *The Noble Eightfold Path.*

> UPADDA SUTTA (SN 45.2),
> *TRANS. BHIKKHU BODHI*

Understanding the "Nonself"

The pain I feel in difficult times is the same pain you feel in difficult times. The circumstances are different, the degree of pain is different, but the basic experience of human suffering is the same.

KRISTEN NEFF AND CHRIS GERMER,
THE MINDFUL SELF-COMPASSION WORKBOOK

Whenever you see someone, consider that, like yourself, that person wants happiness and wants to avoid suffering. We are all the same. We all feel that way. Even the tiniest insect recoils from harm.

BHANTE GUNARATANA, *BEYOND MINDFULNESS*

Early in my studies of Buddhism I was introduced to the three marks of existence, namely, *impermanence*, *unsatisfactoriness*, and *nonself*. They, too, are embedded in a great number of teachings and are reflected in the teaching of the *Four Noble Truths*, so as students we experience numerous exposures to them. Even so, they continue to confuse me.

Through focusing on the breath as we begin meditating, we pay attention to the rising and ceasing of each breath. By doing so we confront the *impermanence* of the breath and subsequently the body.

As my practice has grown, I have learned of the dissatisfaction, disappointment, and suffering that are present in our lives and the role greed plays in their development—so far, an adequate introduction to both *impermanence* and *suffering*.

But when I collided head-on with the notion of the *nonself*, I was introduced to an abstraction that was completely foreign to me. It immediately conjured up many questions about my own identity. "Who am I?" "Is there a soul?" Indeed, "What does 'soul' even mean?" Those questions led to others referring to an afterlife, rebirth, etc.

Many years, discussions, and readings later, I can say that I have progressed to at best a rudimentary understanding of the *nonself*. My best explanation lies within my belief of the *interdependence* of humankind, that we are all of the same family having the same proclivity for kindness alongside the same vulnerability for making some really bad choices.

None of us seems to have mastered the workings of the mind. And nothing in any one of us is terribly unique.

I include this vignette as an example of an early moment when I began to understand our *interdependence*.

"Well, it looks like you got your tit caught in a wringer, this time." That was George—rude, crude, and unapologetic. Normally, I wouldn't be in a relationship with someone like George, but I didn't have the luxury of choice. I was the superintendent of the district where George served on the school board, so we were often in conversations where not only our views, but our personalities, differed. He believed that he was elected to function as a watchdog, representing a segment of the community who by nature distrusted professionals, outsiders, and people who in their eyes weren't worth the salaries they were paid. On all counts, I fit the bill. Strangely, in spite of our differences, we were civil to each other. After much cajoling and discussing education issues, he usually, but begrudgingly, gave in to my position.

This was many years before I began to study Buddhism or had begun to think about the Buddhist concept of the *nonself*, what it means, would I ever make any sense of it. Years later, when reviewing these reminders, the two quotations included above, both linking to the *Noble Truth* of *Right View*, caught my attention and brought George to mind.

Grappling with the notion of *nonself* has been made more challenging because of growing up in a western culture that celebrates our uniqueness as individuals; a culture that encourages individual freedom and independence. All too often, when left unchecked, this mindset can lead us to separate ourselves from the rest of humanity, to compare ourselves to others, to create social norms of excellence, division, and judgment.

The Western emphasis on the individual makes it difficult to embrace the Buddhist notion that there is really nothing about us that is unique or will endure forever and the more we cling to a belief in a unique self, the more we risk being in disharmony with others. And I was frequently in disharmony with George—until we spent time together on a 10-day trip to Japan.

During my last summer serving as a school district superintendent, I, two other administrators, four teachers, George, and one other school board member accompanied nine middle-school students on this trip to Japan. As George explained to me, only once in their 28 years of marriage had he and his wife, Brenda, been away from their dairy farm for a weekend. With cows to milk twice a day, every day, it was just too hard to find anyone to take over the burdens of tending the farm. But George was eager to go on this trip, so managed to find someone to help at home.

We traveled the country, visiting schools and being wined and dined by local dignitaries in our host town of Taichi. George embraced the experience, wanting to learn about Japanese farming, enjoying the Japanese people, and sightseeing. I began to see a different side of him—more open, more curious, more civil. At one point, one of our Japanese hosts asked George, "What do you like to do?"

"Well, I'm a dairy farmer," he replied.

"No, I mean what do you like to do when you aren't farming?"

George had nothing to say about hobbies or interests apart from farming. His silence and discomfort spoke loudly to all there. We could see and feel his unease. Someone came to his rescue, moving the conversation in another direction. But in that brief moment, I felt protective of this gruff man who often challenged me when discussing school district business. With all of his perceived flaws, he was ours. It was painful to see his vulnerability; I didn't like the look on the faces of people who witnessed it.

The following evening, George stood beside me on a hillside overlooking the city of Kyoto. In the quiet of dusk, we were wrapping up a busy day of touring schools and debriefing with our students who were staying with local families. Others were milling about gazing at the view as the lights were beginning to illuminate the city. George was quiet, then turned to me and said, "I wish Brenda were here." The longing in his voice was so poignant, I found no words of response. I haven't forgotten that moment and how his voice had taken on a tone I had never heard from him before.

Two months after returning from our trip, I retired as superintendent and moved on to a university position. I'd like to say that his time in Japan changed George. But according to my successor, it didn't, and really, how presumptuous of me to think it should. But it brings me back to the notion of the *nonself* and its influence on how we perceive others.

When I cling to my sense of self, I am apt to judge others in terms of how their attitudes and actions compare to mine. I create my own standard, proud of my independence.

I see only George, the aggravating contrarian who nitpicks over the most trivial aspects of the school budget, wasting my time and that of other board members during our meetings. Obscured from my vision is George the farmer, the husband; the man who might be longing for other things in life, the chance, perhaps, to give more to his wife.

Here I am 24 years later continuing my efforts to untangle the mysteries of human nature and realize the role of the *nonself* in our search for happiness. I read once more these two quotations that I now treasure and found my thoughts wandering back to that evening in Kyoto, realizing that as we looked out over the city, George and I were not that different. We both wanted to do what was best for the children of our community. We both understood in our own ways the enormity of our responsibility. I'm only now beginning to solidify my belief that *interdependence* among humans is what leads us to successful living. Our *independence* keeps us from understanding and appreciating the different ways we can perceive the world. It kept me from understanding George.

That evening in Kyoto, I took the first steps to comprehending the nature of my ego and the importance of seeing myself in others. The incident occurred without effort or intent on my part. I was not seeking an explanation of my relationship to a particular person or to my fellow humans. But I began then to lay the groundwork for the work I pursue today. The work laid out in the structural framework of *The Four Noble Truths* when the Buddha first claimed that suffering is integral to all life forms.

This work continues to introduce new challenges yet provides opportunities to celebrate minor successes along the way. It goes beyond confronting new notions of reality or arriving at theories I have never before considered. It takes me to the edges of who I am.

The previous vignettes on generosity, spiritual friendship, and *nonself*, followed by the epilogue on equanimity represent examples of how this simple collection of quotations has enriched my awareness of my surroundings. I now offer them to you along with my wish that one of them may provide inspiration or comfort when you need it most.[2]

---

2   Disclaimer: Most of the following quotations have been excerpted from
    readings of mine. Others I have lifted from secondary sources that do not
    include citations. Still others appear in several sources and attribute author
    only. Where possible, I have included complete citations.

Reminder
Quotations

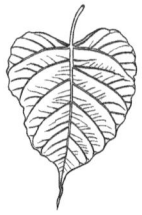

Gratitude is to be cultivated as a habit or
attitude, not dependent on conditions.

K.S. DHAMARATNA,
BUDDHIST MAHA VIHARA, 2019, ALMANAC

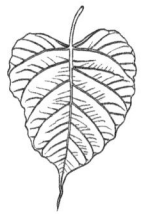

Nibbana (nirvana) is not a location or condition somewhere outside of us. Rather, it is within. The very moment our greed, hatred, and ignorance are destroyed, nibbana arises.

BHANTE GUNARATANA,
MEDITATION ON PERCEPTION

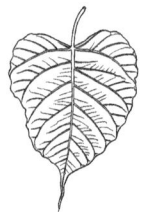

The torments of hell as well as the
joys of heaven, no matter how long
they will last, are bound to pass.

BHIKKHU BODHI, IN THE BUDDHA'S WORDS

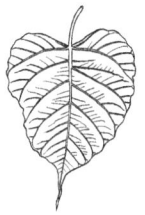

If you harm a pure and innocent person,
you harm yourself, as dust thrown against
the wind comes back to the thrower.

THE BUDDHA, *THE DHAMMAPADA*

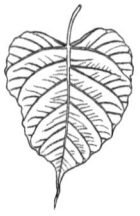

The mind is its own place…and in itself can
make a heaven of hell or hell of heaven.

JOHN MILTON, *PARADISE LOST*

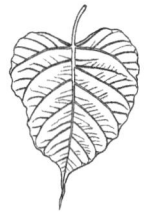

Only we humans worry about the
future, regret the past, and blame
ourselves for the present.

RICK HANSON AND RICHARD MENDIUS, *BUDDHA'S BRAIN*

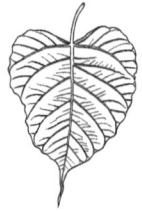

Appreciation is a wonderful
thing. It makes what is excellent
in others belong to us as well.

VOLTAIRE

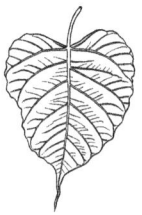

Thoughts manifest as actions, which in
turn develop into habits, and our habits
ultimately harden into character.

FRANK OSTESESKI,
THE FIVE INVITATIONS (AND OTHERS)

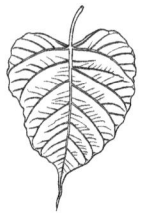

Forgiveness is not an occasional act;
it is a constant attitude.

MARTIN LUTHER KING, JR.

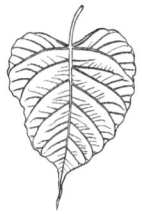

Discovering more joy does not save
us from the inevitability of hardship
and heartbreak…as we discover more
joy, we can face suffering in a way that
ennobles rather than embitters. We have
hardship without becoming hard. We have
heartbreak without being broken.

DESMOND TUTU

Wisdom is purified by virtue, and virtue is purified by wisdom. Where one is, so is the other. The virtuous person has wisdom, and the wise person has virtue. The combination of virtue and wisdom is called the highest thing in the world.

THE BUDDHA, *DIGHA NIKAYA*

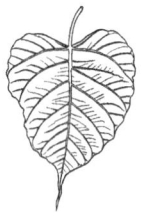

People have a hard time letting go of their
suffering. Out of a fear of the unknown, they
prefer suffering that is familiar.

THICH NHAT HANH

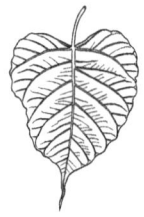

The torments of hell as well as the joys of heaven, no matter how long they will last, are bound to pass.

BHIKKHU BODHI, *IN THE BUDDHA'S WORDS*

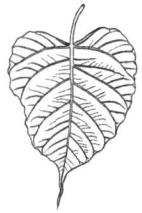

In Buddhism, loving kindness, or *metta*, is
considered a sublime state of being.
A heavenly realm. It's expansive, allowing,
caring, and connective. Attachment
masquerades as love. It looks and smells
like love, but it's a cheap imitation…love is
selfless, attachment is self-centered. Love is
freeing, attachment is possessive. When we
love, we relax, we don't hold on so tightly,
and we naturally let go more easily.

FRANK OSTESESKI, *5 INVITATIONS*

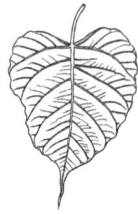

Generosity brings happiness at every stage of its expression: we experience joy in forming the intention to give, we experience joy in the action of giving, and we experience joy in remembering that we have given.

BETH ROTH, *FAMILY DHAMMA: THE JOY OF GENEROSITY*

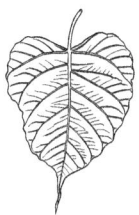

The wise live without injuring nature, as the bee drinks nectar without harming the flower.

THE BUDDHA, *THE DHAMMAPADA*

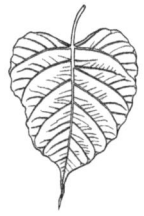

We cannot watch a breath that is past;
nor one yet in the future. We can only
watch the one that is happening.

AYYA KHEMA, *WHEN THE IRON EAGLE FLIES*

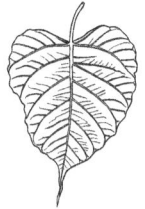

I did not begin My Buddhist practice with
any intention to discover my body...Slowly
over the years as my body has begun to
come alive, I was, and still am, repeatedly
surprised by how much awareness, love,
and compassion are found in and through
the body. I have learned that mindfulness of
the body is the foundation of mindfulness
practice, and one of the best friends for
integrating that practice into daily life.

GIL FRONSDALE, *THE INQUIRING MIND*

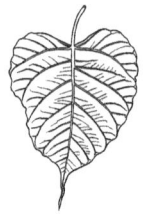

It takes courage to grow up and
turn out to be who you really are.

E.E.CUMMINGS, *LOVE IS A PLACE*

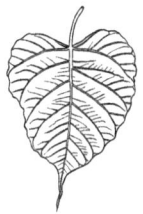

You cannot step into the same river twice.

HERACLITIS, GREEK PHILOSOPHER

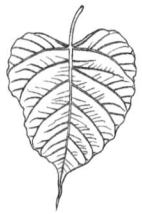

Generosity has such power because
it is characterized by the inner
quality of letting go or relinquishing.

SHARON SALZBERG, *LOVING KINDNESS*

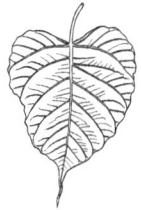

As we become aware of the feelings in us, our self-understanding will deepen. We will see how our fears and lack of peace contribute to our unhappiness, and we will see the value of loving ourselves and cultivating a heart of compassion.

THICH NHAT HANH, *CULTIVATING COMPASSION*

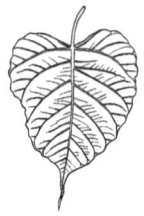

You will not be punished for your anger;
you will be punished by your anger.

THE BUDDHA, *THE DHAMMAPADA*

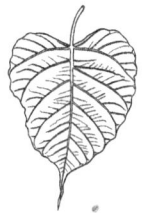

Meditation is a patient process of knowing
that gradually over time, habits are dissolving.
We don't actually get rid of anything.
We are just steadfast with ourselves,
developing clearer awareness and becoming
honest about who we are and what we do.

PEMA CHODRON, *MAKING FRIENDS WITH ONESELF*

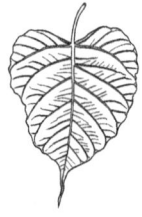

Holding on to anger is like grasping a hot coal
with the intent of throwing it at someone else.
You are the one who gets burned.

THE BUDDHA, *THE DHAMMAPADA*

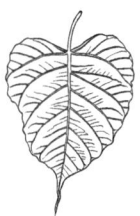

When there is quarrelsome talk, much
talk may be expected, when there is much
talk one is excited, being excited one is
uncontrolled, and when one is uncontrolled
the mind is far from concentrated.

THE BUDDHA, *ANGUTTARA NIKAYA IV, 87*

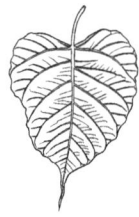

Whatever one thinks about and ponders over often, one's mind gets a leaning in that way.

THE BUDDHA, *MAJJIHIMA NIKAYA I, 115*

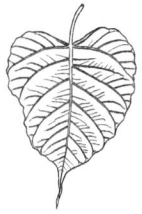

To cultivate equanimity we practice catching
ourselves when we feel attraction or aversion,
before it hardens into grasping or negativity.

PEMA CHODRON

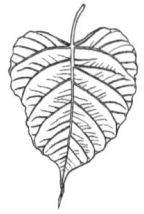

The mind, by its very nature, is not
dark, murky, or turbulent. In its essential
character it has light; it is bright, filled
with shining, open, non-conceptual
intelligence, and a deep tranquility.

BHANTE GUNARATANA, *BEYOND MINDFULNESS*

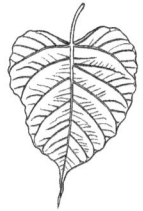

Luminosity refers to the mind's ability to see when its actions are defiled, and to train itself to act in ways that are undefiled and pure.

THANISSARO BHIKKHU, *METTA MEANS GOODWILL*

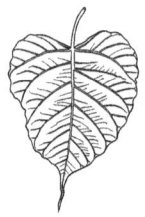

Meditation practice is not about trying to throw ourselves away and become something better, it's about befriending who we are.

ANI PEMA CHODRON

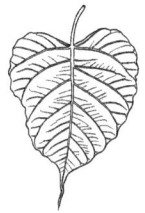

Learn this from the waters;
In mountain clefts and chasms,
Loud gushes the streamlets,
But great rivers flow silently.

Empty things make a noise
The full is always quiet.
The fool is like a half-filled pot,
The wise one is like a deep, still pool.

THE BUDDHA, *NIPATHA SUTTA*

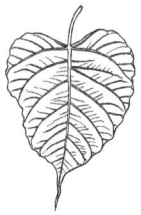

Anger limits us. But if we have the courage to
look at our anger and its causes and to learn
from it, we can develop an open heart –
a heart of genuine compassion.

JULES SHUZEN HARRIS,
UPROOTING THE SEEDS OF ANGER

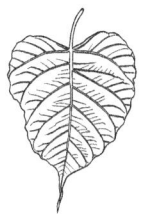

The real issue in life is not how many blessings we have, but what we do with our blessings. Some people have many blessings and hoard them. Some have few and give everything away.

FRED ROGERS

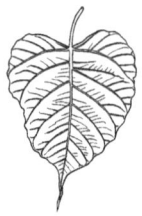

Whatever harm an enemy may do to an
enemy, or a hater to a hater, an ill-directed
mind inflicts on oneself greater harm.

THE BUDDHA, *THE DHAMMAPADA*

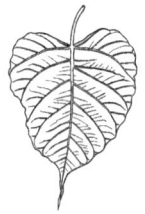

Not seeing that our problems are within us, we are like a dog with fleas. Unable to get comfortable in one place, the dog moves to another place thinking there are no fleas there.

THUBTEN CHODRON,
BUDDHISM: ONE TEACHER, MANY TRADITIONS

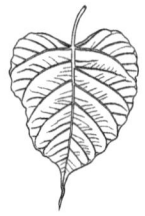

As iron sharpens iron, so one
person sharpens another.

<small>PROVERBS 27:17, *THE BIBLE*</small>

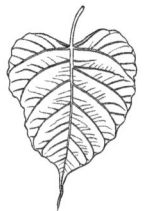

Your brain is like Velcro for negative
experiences and Teflon for positive
experiences – even though most of your
experiences are either neutral or positive.

RICK HANSON AND RICHARD MENDIUS,
BUDDHA'S BRAIN

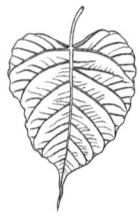

A spoon of salt in a glass of water
makes the water undrinkable. A spoon
of salt in a lake is almost unnoticed.

THE BUDDHA

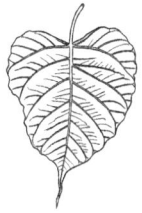

If we could read the secret history of
our enemies, we would find in each
person's life sorrow and suffering
enough to disarm any hostility.

HENRY WADSWORTH LONGFELLOW

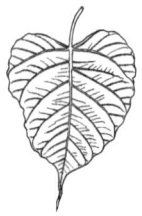

I make myself rich by making my wants few.

HENRY DAVID THOREAU, *WALDEN*

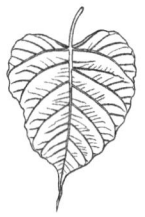

There is no use wishing harm to someone who is bringing harm upon himself. It is better to generate compassion for him.

THUBTEN CHODRON,
BUDDHISM: ONE TEACHER, MANY TRADITIONS

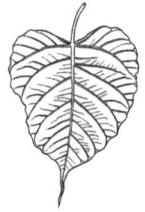

We can make ourselves miserable or
we can make ourselves strong. The
amount of effort is the same.

PEMA CHODRON

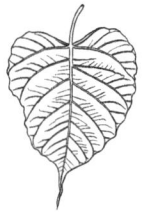

The meditation you do on the
cushion is your homework; the rest
of your life is your fieldwork; to
practice mindfulness you need both.

BHANTE GUNARATANA,
THE FOUR FOUNDATIONS OF MINDFULNESS

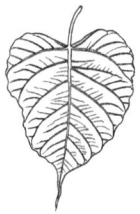

He who puts aside his wants in order
to do the right thing, even though it
be difficult, is like a patient drinking
medicine. Later he will rejoice.

THE BUDDHA, *JATAKA*

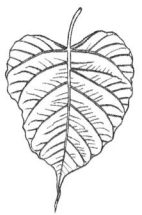

Remember that in letting go of distraction,
the important word is "gentle." We can
gently let go; we can forgive ourselves for
having wandered, and with great kindness to
ourselves, we can begin again.

SHARON SALZBERG

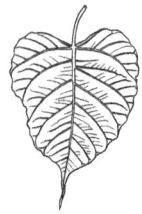

We must think about our choices of words before they come out of our mouths and that is difficult…just as we do not or should not swear in public or in private, I pledge to add the word {hate} to the collection of four-letter expletives I will not use. The H word is an extreme word and extreme language will usually lead to extreme action.

RABBI JEFFREY MYERS, *TREE OF LIFE SYNAGOGUE*

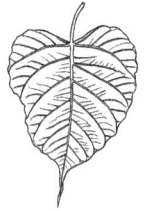

It isn't the things that happen to us
in our lives that cause us to suffer;
it's how we relate to the things that
happen to us that cause us to suffer.

PEMA CHODRON

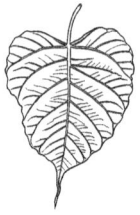

Fear keeps us focused on the past or
worried about the future. If we can
acknowledge our fear, we can realize
that right now we are okay.

THICH NHAT HANH

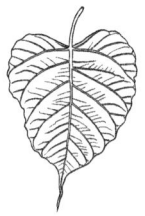

The fact is that when you make the other suffer, he will try to find relief by making you suffer more. The result is an escalation of suffering on both sides.

THICH NHAT HANH,
ANGER: WISDOM FOR COOLING THE FLAMES

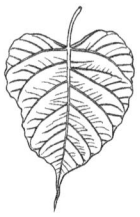

What people expect to happen is often
different from what actually happens.
Thus does disappointment arise. This
is the way the world works.

THE BUDDHA, *SUTTA NIPATA*

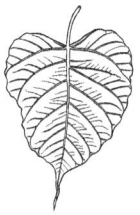

Most people bring less kindness to
themselves than to others.

RICK HANSON AND RICHARD MENDIUS, *BUDDHA'S BRAIN*

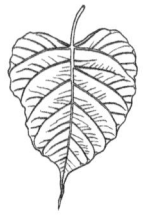

The *sangha* is a refuge because those who have preceded us on the path can give us advice on the journey ahead, while those who are walking with us can provide companionship on the journey, bring us back to the path when we deviate, and help us up when we stumble and fall.

THE BUDDHA, *FROM THE TIPITAKA*

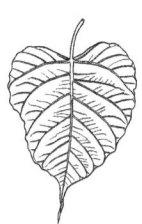

You don't need to be an "excellent meditator" to start with. All you need to do is have your heart and mind make the following agreement: 'Let's rest." There's no reason right now to wander around following thoughts or worrying. Let's be relaxed and open.

DZA KILUNG RIMPOCHE, *THE RELAXED MIND*

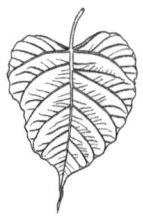

If you can be happy when good things
happen to other people, your opportunities
for delight are increased by eight billion.

THE DALAI LAMA

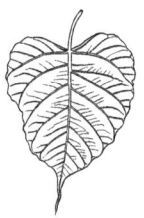

Just as a solid rock is not shaken by
the wind, even so, the wise are not
affected by praise or blame.

THE BUDDHA, *THE DHAMMAPADA*

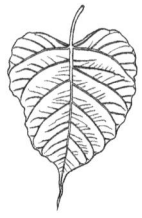

The outside world offers us a testing ground
where we can check on and mature the
insights gained in formal meditation. We need
to avoid creating a rigid division between
formal meditation and ordinary activities.

BHIKKHU ANALAYO,
SATIPATTHANA MEDITATION: A PRACTICE GUIDE

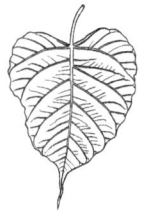

Sympathetic joy is the heartfelt
gratification that accompanies
the awareness of another's well-
being. It's a joy entirely devoid
of expectations. Instead, it carries
one of life's greatest pleasures:
celebrating the happiness of others.

ELLEN AGLER, *IN THE SPIRIT OF SERVICE*

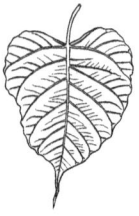

The difference between misery and happiness
depends on what we do with our attention.

SHARON SALZBERG

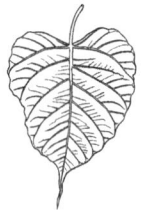

I have learned through bitter experience
the one supreme lesson is to conserve
my anger, and as heat conserved is
transmuted into energy; our anger
controlled can be transmuted into a
power which can change the world.

MAHATMA GANDHI

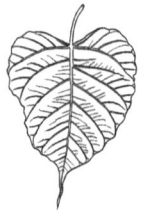

The bittersweet side of appreciating life's
most precious moments is the unbearable
awareness that those moments are passing.

MARC PARENT

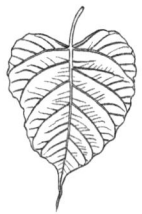

The quality of human life on our planet is
nothing more than the sum total of our daily
interactions with one another. Each time
we help and each time we harm, we have a
dramatic impact on our world.

DESMOND TUTU

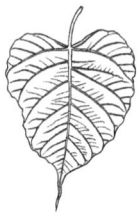

Our minds are vulnerable to addiction if we
do not develop an inner source of satisfaction.

BHANTE PEMARATANA,
DHAMMA BLOG, PITTSBURGH BUDDHIST CENTER

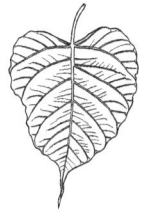

May that which is still be that in
which your mind delights.

RICK HANSEN

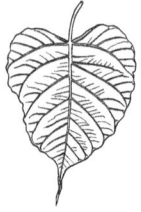

To cultivate our equanimity, we practice
catching ourselves when we feel
attraction or aversion before it hardens
into grasping or negativity.

PEMA CHODRON

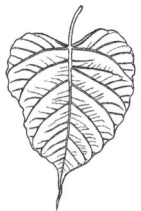

Where is the path…it is within us…
we will never find the path anywhere
else – not in books, not in a shop, not in
temples. It is within us. Mindfulness is
the key that opens the gate to this road.

BHANTE GUNARATANA,
MEDITATION ON PERCEPTION

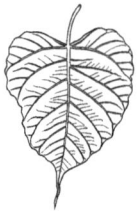

To be present is the most fundamental
generosity of all. When there is nothing
else to do, when we are in a situation that
seems hopelessly blocked, there is still one
thing we can do: we can be there.

LEWIS RICHMOND, *WORK IS A SPIRITUAL PRACTICE*

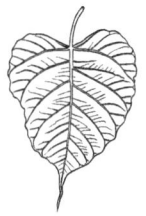

You should sit in meditation for 20 minutes a day unless you are busy, then you should sit for an hour.

ZEN SAYING

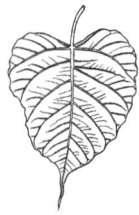

Not getting what you desire and getting what
you desire can both be disappointing.

THE BUDDHA

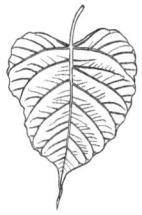

The pain I feel in difficult times is the same pain you feel in difficult times. The circumstances are different, the degree of pain is different, but the basic experience of human suffering is the same.

KRISTEN NEFF AND CHRIS GERMER,
THE MINDFUL SELF-COMPASSION WORKBOOK

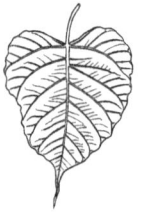

A sigh, after all, is an outbreath with
a story attached to it. By expelling it,
we make space for a new one.

LESLIE GARRETT,
WHAT SCIENCE SAYS ABOUT THE POWER OF THE OUTBREATH

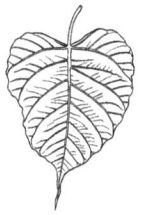

The disease of men is that they neglect their own fields and go to weed the fields of others.

MENCIUS

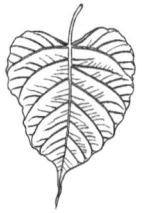

There is no boundary between us and our environment, which is both other people and the whole of the natural world. So if we want a less polluted environment, it will depend on a less polluted mind…

AYYA KHEMA, *WHO IS MYSELF*

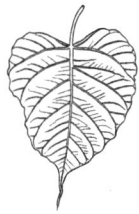

Equanimity is the hallmark of
spirituality. It is neither chasing nor
avoiding but just being in the middle.

AMIT RAY, *MEDITATION: INSIGHTS AND INSPIRATIONS*

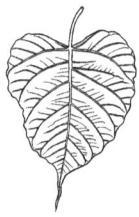

Before you embark on a journey
of revenge, dig two graves.

<small>CONFUCIUS</small>

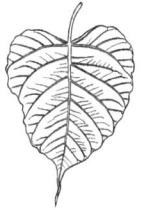

The one who conquers himself, the victor
over his own mind, achieves a conquest
that can never be undone, a victory greater
than that of the mightiest warriors.

THE BUDDHA, *THE DHAMMAPADA*

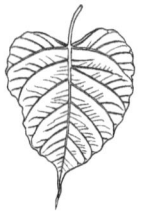

This is my simple religion. There is no
need for temples, no need for complicated
philosophy. Our own brain, our own heart is
our temple; the philosophy is kindness.

THE DALAI LAMA

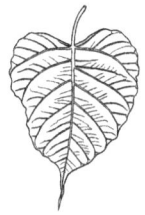

Whenever you see someone, consider
that, like yourself, that person wants
happiness and wants to avoid suffering.
We are all the same. We all feel that way.
Even the tiniest insect recoils from harm.

BHANTE GUNARATANA, *BEYOND MINDFULNESS*

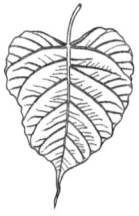

The inevitable suffering of human life is relieved by awareness, not by avoidance, suppression or distraction.

BETH JACOBS,
THE ORIGINAL BUDDHIST PSYCHOLOGY

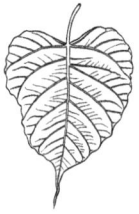

Apply yourself to solitude. One who is given
to solitude knows things as they really are.

THE BUDDHA, *SAMYUTTA NIKAYA*

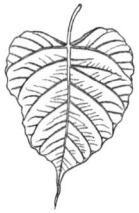

There are two days in the year that we cannot
do anything, yesterday and tomorrow.

MAHATMA GANDHI

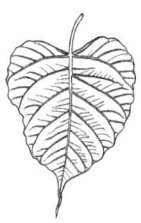

When one happily shares or gives up the best one has, whether it be time, energy, or material resources, that is princely giving.

KENNETH KRAFT,
THE WHEEL OF ENGAGED BUDDHISM

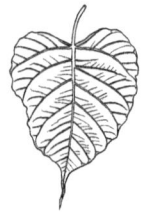

To end our suffering, we must end
our attachment to things that are
constantly changing.

BHANTE GUNARATANA, *MEDITATION ON PERCEPTION*

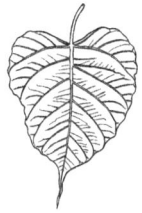

...people will become truly happy not as a result of your caring for them but as a result of their own skillful actions, and the happiness of self-reliance is greater than the happiness that comes from dependency.

THANISSARO BHIKKHU, *METTA MEANS GOODWILL*

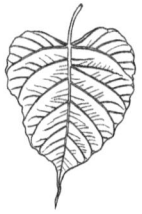

I have decided to stick with love;
hate is too great a burden to bear.

<small>MARTIN LUTHER KING, JR.</small>

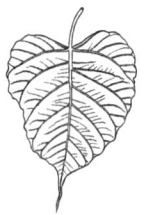

By effort and heedfulness, discipline and self-mastery, the wise one makes for himself an island which no flood can overwhelm.

THE BUDDHA, *THE DHAMMAPADA*

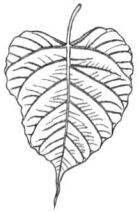

There comes a point where we need
to stop just pulling people out of the
river. We need to go upstream and
find out why they're falling in.

DESMOND TUTU

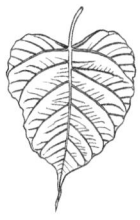

I need time for my confusion. Confusion can be a cue that there's new territory to be explored or a fresh puzzle to be solved.

ADAM GRANT,
*THINK AGAIN: THE POWER OF
KNOWING WHAT YOU DON'T KNOW*

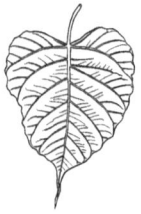

This concentration on in and out breathing,
if cultivated and developed, is something
peaceful and excellent, something perfect
in itself and a pleasant way of living also.
More than that it dispels evil thoughts that
have arisen and makes them vanish in a
moment. It is just as when, in the last month
of the hot season, the dust and the dirt fly up
and suddenly a great shower of rain lays it
and makes it settle in a moment.

THE BUDDHA, *SAMYUTTA NIKAYA*

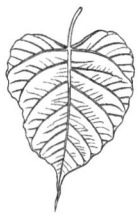

Just as an arrow-maker straightens an
arrow shaft, even so the discerning person
straightens his mind – so fickle and unsteady,
so difficult to guard and control.

THE BUDDHA, *THE DHAMMAPADA*

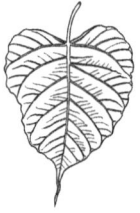

It is unwise to be too sure of one's own wisdom. It is healthy to be reminded that the strongest might weaken and the wisest might err.

MAHATMA GANDHI

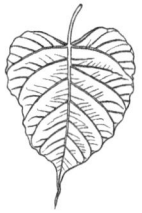

It is not happiness that makes us grateful;
it is gratefulness that makes us happy.

STEINDL – RAST, BENEDICTINE MONK

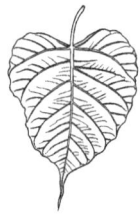

When we practice meditation, we are doing something useful for all beings…with the experience of greater clarity, we learn how to bring happiness into our pathway and can engage in meaningful actions for discovering and digging up gold from the earth.

DZA KILUNG RINPOCHE, *THE RELAXED MIND*

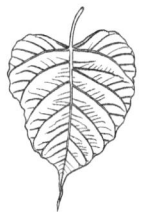

You are not only responsible for what you say,
but also for what you do not say.

MARTIN LUTHER

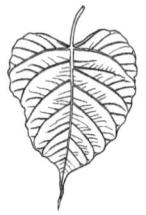

Pain is certain,
Suffering is optional.

THE BUDDHA

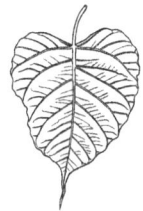

The heart needs training because by nature it isn't alway constituted to feel loving kindness. By nature it contains both love and hate. It contains ill will, rejection, resentment and fear, but also love. Unless we diminish the hate, and enlarge the love by doing something about it in our daily life, we have no chance of experiencing that peaceful feeling that loving kindness generates in the heart. It's a skill. It's not an inbred character fault or ability.

AYYA KHEMA, *BEING NOBODY, GOING NOWHERE*

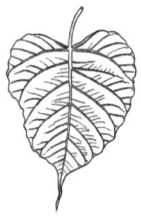

There may be no greater sense of
fulfillment in life than the simultaneous
feelings of human interconnection
and pure freedom that arise from an
authentic act of selfless generosity.

DALE S. WRIGHT, *THE BODHISATTVA'S GIFT*

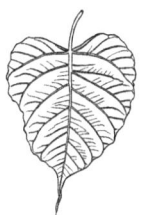

Even when, or maybe especially when, it seems like blessings are few, that may be the most important time to count them.

AMY MORIN FORBES, *THE POWER OF GRATITUDE*

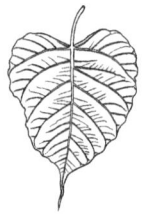

The greatest beneficiary of your
forgiveness is usually you.

JACK KORNFIELD,
THE ART OF FORGIVENESS,
LOVING KINDNESS, AND PEACE

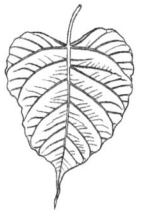

The curious paradox is that when I accept
myself just as I am, then I can change.

CARL ROGERS

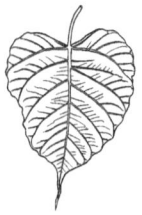

If we learn to let go into uncertainty, to trust
that our basic nature and that of the world
are not different, then the fact that things are
not solid and fixed becomes, rather than a
threat, a liberating opportunity.

CAROL HYMAN,
LIVING AND DYING: A BUDDHIST PERSPECTIVE

Epilogue

*The torments of hell as well as the joys
of heaven, no matter how long they
will last, are bound to pass.*

BHIKKHU BODHI, *IN THE BUDDHA'S WORDS*

*To cultivate our equanimity, we practice catching
ourselves when we feel attraction or aversion
before it hardens into grasping or negativity.*

PEMA CHODRON

On a crisp, October afternoon in 2011, I knelt on the lawn of the Pittsburgh Buddhist Center in front of a delegation of seven visiting and resident monks. As friends and fellow practitioners looked on, I vowed to lead my life in accordance with the precepts that the Buddha had handed down for lay followers. I took refuge in the Buddha, the *Dhamma*, and the *Sangha*, pledging my intention to grow in my practice.

Part of the ceremony included the monks giving me my Buddhist name…*Upekha*. Bhante Pema shared that the name in Pali means "equanimity." At the time, I was unsure what equanimity meant, and I have spent many hours since that afternoon wondering about its meaning.

Few westerners in our Sangha go by their Buddhist names, but since that day, Bhante Pema and several of my Sri Lankan friends refer to me as Upekha. I am deeply humbled to carry it as part of my Buddhist identity.

I was not sure why he chose it for me. I vacillated between thinking maybe I exhibited some signs of it…or more likely, that he thought my lack of it was a weakness I needed to work on. Over the years I've become less concerned about why I was given the name and more interested in understanding its meaning.

Simply put, equanimity means accepting life as it unfolds. Knowing that the easy times will not last. Nor will the bad. It means curtailing exuberance over accomplishments and quietly persevering in the face of suffering and travail. We learn to accept the difficulties and pay attention when all is well, knowing we can fall prey to the dangers of excess. Too often we have seen examples of those whose success has led to lives of utter destruction.

The Buddha encourages a middle path existence. Kind of a "this too will pass" mentality, like Bhikkhu Bodhi lays out in the first quotation above.

But like most Buddhist concepts, it presents itself as simple, yet with further examination reveals its complexity. At one point in my effort to better understand it, I discovered the notion of "near and far enemies." I've since come across that phrase in a few psychology texts, but its origin, I believe, is found in Buddhist writings. It has helped me understand the nuances of equanimity.

For example, the far enemy of love is its opposite, hatred. On the other hand, the near enemy of love is craving and attachment. Attachment resembles love, but it represents a distorted version that is harmful and causes suffering. It reminds us of the parent whose love is transformed into control, control that restricts a child well into adulthood. On the surface, it might pass for love, but is damaging and painful to both parties in its extreme.

"Near and far enemies" most often appear in reference to the four "divine abodes," which we know as loving kindness *(metta)*, compassion *(corona)*, sympathetic joy *(mudita)*, and equanimity *(upekha)*. In order to experience equanimity, the ultimate among the four, we must first have accomplished skill in the three former states. On the surface, I thought I had a fundamental understanding of equanimity until I began to apply it to my own behavior.

I see how I could fall into that trap of controlling, the near enemy of love. Fortunately, my adult children are strong enough that they immediately temper any attempts I might make to control their actions. For that I am thankful.

The far enemy of our efforts to remain calm and balanced is its opposite, excitement. The near enemy is indifference. It might look like equanimity, balanced and non-emotional, but lacks the compassion that characterizes equanimity. Think of the hospice worker who accepts the oncoming death of a patient with calmness. She shows minimal emotion when treating the dying person but exhibits deep compassion and gentleness while guiding him through the process. That is equanimity. When compassion is absent, it is simply indifference.

The second quotation, by Pema Chodron, provides a practical application of mindfulness that has helped broaden my understanding of equanimity and even better, actually translates into a means of changing behavior. If, through our meditation, we are developing the ability to observe our minds and ultimately influence them to avoid extreme emotions, this seems a more doable explanation of how someone might cultivate equanimity. Over the years, viewing my behavior in the mirror of Buddhist concepts has become a major thrust of my practice. I have developed an ongoing desire to know how I stack up and what I need to do to better understand my actions and thoughts.

As Bhante Pema once explained to our Tuesday meditation group, we don't come upon extreme emotion in one leap. For example, we might begin with an uneasy feeling of disruption which can lead to a more intense feeling of annoyance followed by a deepening feeling of anger, possibly from there becoming a feeling of rage. That entire transition can take place in a minute or less.

When we are able to intervene, perhaps at the onset of feeling annoyed, we might be able to cut off the oncoming anger at will. This is mindfulness in action. And it is through such mindfulness that we can actually help ourselves reach that calm, balanced state of equanimity.

This kind of intervention is not easy to perform in the heat of the moment. There have been innumerable times when I have stopped myself after saying or doing something I wish I hadn't, wondering why I didn't catch myself before doing so.

My search for a deeper understanding of equanimity began before I started collecting quotations. But once I began the collection of quotations and my personal reflections that accompanied them, the connections became apparent. Pema Chodron's quote along with Bhante's explanation are both examples of connecting the teachings to my behavior and real events.

It is now becoming clear to me that most of my discomfort originates with ideas or people that I am attached to and that the ego that compels me to control events around me is at the center of many conflicts in my mind.

Through these sustained reflections on specific quotations, I have learned to see and feel new relevance in *The Four Noble Truths* alongside examples of equanimity and other major Buddhist concepts. They are no longer simply academic pursuits.

Compiling these quotations has been a joy for me. It has given me an opportunity to study in an unexpected way, a way that led me from concept to concept, experience to experience. Undirected by anyone, the quotations randomly transported me to places I needed to visit.

I would say that I probably know more about Buddhism now, or maybe it's better to say that I know more about myself through Buddhism now than when I started.

My friend, Maria, encouraged me to complete this work when I began to wonder if anyone would find it interesting. She provided one more important reminder for me. Writing it for myself was reason enough to continue.

So, this journey lives on with me, my thoughts, readings, meditation, contact with these monks...and yes, the quotations, my reminders that I share with you.

About the Author

Sue Goodwin spent over 40 years of her professional life as an education practitioner. Whether a teacher, administrator, curriculum designer, leader of leaders, or consultant, her most important role always remained that of learner. Earning a PhD in Curriculum and Supervision, she was an ardent advocate for public education, always probing into ways to improve her own personal understanding of how learning best occurs. This pursuit continues today in retirement as she discovers the wonders of Buddhism and how our varied efforts to understand it can lead us to a new definition of happiness.

Learning Moments Press

Learning Moments Press is the publishing arm of the Scholar-Practitioner Nexus, an online community of individuals committed to the quality of education. Learning Moments Press features three series of books.

The Wisdom of Practice Series showcases the work of individuals who illuminate the complexities of practice as they strive to fulfill the purpose of their profession.

The Wisdom of Life Series offers insightful reflections on significant life events that challenge the meaning of one's life, one's sense of self, and one's place in the world.

The Social Context Series showcases the work of individuals who illuminate the macro socio-economic-political contexts within which education policy and practice are enacted.

Cooligraphy artist Daniel Nie created the logo for Learning Moments Press by combining two symbol systems. Following the principles of ancient Asian symbols, Daniel framed the logo with the initials of Learning Moments Press. Within this frame, he has replicated the Adinkra symbol for *Sankofa* as interpreted by graphic artists at the Documents and Design Company. As explained by Wikipedia, Adinkra is a writing system of the Akan culture of West Africa. *Sankofa* symbolizes taking from the past what is good and bringing it into the present in order to make positive progress through the benevolent use of knowledge. Inherent in this philosophy is the belief that the past illuminates the present and that the search for knowledge is a life-long process.